ESTABLISH A
SUPER
SUCCESSFUL
MINI DAIRY
PROCESSING BUSINESS

The 4 Pillars to an Unerring Reliable Dairy Business Revealed!

ESTABLISH A
SUPER
SUCCESSFUL
MINI DAIRY
PROCESSING BUSINESS

The 4 Pillars to an Unerring Reliable Dairy Business Revealed!

AMARDEEP SINGH CHADHA

Worldwide Published by

Pendown Press

PENDOWN PRESS
An ISO 9001 & ISO 14001 Certified Co.,
Regd. Office: 2525/193, 1st Floor, Onkar Nagar-A,
Tri Nagar, Delhi-110035
Ph.: 09350849407, 09312235086
E-mail: info@pendownpress.com
Branch Office: 1A/2A, 20, Hari Sadan, Ansari Road,
Daryaganj, New Delhi-110002
Ph.: 011-45794768
Website: PendownPress.com

First Edition: 2023

ISBN: 978-93-5554-476-6

Layout and Cover Designed by Pendown Graphics Team
Printed and Bound in India by Thomson Press India Ltd.

*I dedicate this book to my
Grandfather, Late Sardar Makhan
Singh Chadha, whose eternal
blessings are upon us and on his
created foundation we stand.*

Contents

Acknowledgements

The world is indeed a better place, thanks to people who develop and support others. What makes it even better is the people who share the gift of their time, knowledge and experience to mentor future leaders. Thank you to everyone who strives to grow and help society and humanity grow and develop as a whole.

Nobody has been more important to me in the pursuit of this project than my parents, Sdn. Surjeet Kaur and S. MPS Chadha, whose love and guidance are with me in whatever I pursue. Thank you, Mom and Dad, for your love, prayers, care and continuing support for educating and instilling optimum values and the finest virtues for preparing me to ensure the best future. You are the ultimate role model for me.

Most importantly, I wish to thank my loving and supportive wife, Kavleen, for keeping the munchkins out of my hair so I could write wholeheartedly. She was as important to this book getting done as I was. Thank you for always being there and supporting me on my latest hare-brained scheme.

Loads of thanks to my wonderful children, Anika and Praneet, without whom my life is joyless. Their selfless love and affection are the fuel that provides unending inspiration to me for a beautiful future ahead.

Writing a book is harder than I thought and more rewarding than I could have ever imagined. None of this would have been possible without the support of my brothers, dear Manjeet and dear Jagdeep. They stood by me during every struggle and all my successes. That is the literal Brotherhood.

I'm eternally grateful to my uncle S. Baldev Singh Chadha. He taught me discipline, love, respect, and so much more that have helped me succeed in life. I truly have no idea where I'd be without his parasol over my head, the father figure whom I desperately admire. One can not do anything without the support of family. I have one, and it's a great fortune. I thank the almighty for that.

Without the experiences and support from my team at Chadha Sales Private Limited, this book would not exist. You have given me the opportunity to lead a great group of individuals—to be a leader of great leaders is a blessed place to be.

Thank you Mr. J.M Saluja, whose support and guidance have crafted the path of writing this book. Thank you, Ms. Rubi Kumari, for being supportive of my ventures and thank you, Ms. Ritu Gupta, for managing my schedule, which has given me time to express myself.

Acknowledgements

Foremost, how can I miss thanking all my clients whom I have served over the last so many years and who shared with me the ground realities of business and became the very base that encouraged me to write this book.

A very special word of gratitude to Arsh, Palav, Jenit & Banni; you are a joy to my heart and a delight to my eyes.

Last but not least: I can not express enough thanks to all my nearer & dearer ones who have been with me over the course of the years and whose names are not mentioned in this book because the list lying in my heart is endlessly long and needs a separate book in fact. I apologise for this to the core. In one or the other way, you all are actually the inspiring and guiding force behind all my endeavours.

Above all, I thank the Universe for generating this idea and providing an environment to write and share my knowledge and experience with all of you and keeping me focused until the end of the book.

Amardeep Singh Chadha

Who Should Read this Book?

This book is specially intended for aspiring entrepreneurs aiming to enter the dairy industry and create a buzz. It will be instrumental in helping them navigate the challenges of the dairy business smoothly and successfully to survive and thrive in this sector.

It would also help existing dairy entrepreneurs, especially micro, small and medium size dairies. This book will motivate dairy enterprises struggling to grow and show them a different path to success.

It will also prove extremely useful for dairy farmers who would like to sell their products directly to consumers and also for people who are into milk collection and would like to venture into the milk processing business.

In a nutshell, whoever dreams of having an enterprise related to milk and milk products should read this book.

How to use this Book?

Do not just pay attention to the words; Instead pay attention to meanings behind the words.

But, do not just pay attention to meanings behind the words; Instead pay attention to the deep experience of those meanings.

~Tenzin Gyatso, The Fourteenth Dalai Lama

This book is intended to change your perspective of the dairy business. If you are planning to or thinking of entering into the dairy industry, this is a must-read for you.

It will help you understand that there is and will be prospective growth in the dairy sector and how you can be prepared to leverage that opportunity by understanding the challenges you might encounter on entering or moving forward in this huge industry.

This book will show you the foundational requirement for establishing and sustaining a successful dairy enterprise. I am sure you will research and explore a lot before entering into the same, but everything is not shared everywhere. No one really shares the critical inside information to give you a factual picture of the industry.

Some of the problems related to the industry are difficult to even visualize in your head, so obviously, then, their answers are unimaginable. Here you need a super-experienced expert to handhold you through the process.

This book is your go-to expert. It has all the answers to difficulties and incomprehension.

It will help you like an immensely experienced Grandee or a Veteran guiding you and build your self-confidence to troubleshoot the challenges that crop up. With this book, you will be able to:

- Identify your real difficulties regarding your work.

- Find solutions and proofs to propel you forward to success

- Receive answers to the numerous questions crowding your mind

This book will function as your starting point; once you go through the chapters in their entirety, you should continue on your quest for further learning in this industry. We recommend that after going through this book, you should opt for a deeper knowledge of the domain further. You will find the golden opportunity when you complete this book with a gift at the end.

Introduction

Let's begin at the beginning when I completed my studies abroad and joined my family business. It was a great life; selling dairy machines and instruments and making money was great fun. I spent many comfortable and prosperous years within the confines of my company. I had never taken the opportunity to venture outside to see my customers and explore the dairy industry in general.

In 2008 we started delivering turnkey dairies to entrepreneurs who wanted to start a dairy business. Thereafter my interaction with dairy enterprises increased a little. Although I was manufacturing machinery side by side, I was witnessing and learning from the entrepreneurship journeys of many dairy entrepreneurs, and I witnessed both successes and failures.

Whenever I heard about a dairy failure, it was heartbreaking for me, and I always felt very frustrated and upset. And one question that kept bothering me was this:

"Why do dairy enterprises fail?"

India is a country of milk lovers, and milk is in abundance. There is a huge consumer base in India, and the dairy business is fairly profitable, but still, some succeed and some fail in this business.

Sadly, I could find no answer to that!

I am sure you must have also often heard that this or that known dairy had closed down as they failed to sustain their business. Each time I learned about a dairy business failure anywhere across India, I would be inquisitive about the reasons behind its failure.

As per my calculation dairy business should not fail at all as it has the potential for a great ROI, and dairy is a science which can be thoroughly understood and then practiced.

There are so many dairy science experts available. But still, there are failures. This query remained embedded somewhere in the back of my mind for many years. But I was fully occupied with my business, so I could not spare any time to analyse it and work on it.

In 2020 Covid came in uninvited, and everyone's life was suspended. As I am a workaholic, I became really worried as to what I would do if I had to stay closed at one place for an indefinite time period.

Then came the day when the whole world shut down due to the pandemic. My office and factories had to come to a stop along with the rest of the world.

It was the momentous first day of the lockdown. Suddenly in the morning, I was struck by an idea!

I thought, why don't I spend my time constructively working on, researching and resolving my long pending pain related to the mysteries of dairy failure?

Finally, through a strange set of circumstances, the Universe gifted me my purpose. I decided that I would put all my energy into this task and take advantage of this time to resolve this gruesome query and find a way to help dairy enterprises in these challenging pandemic-ridden times. I started my endeavor from that very day. When there is a thirst and a sacred intent in your soul to seek something, the universe provides a path.

I had many case studies already in my records, and as I began studying them in-depth, slowly and steadily, I was able to put my finger on the reason for the frequent dairy failures.

And to my surprise, the reasons behind these failures were not complicated. They were occurring for basic, fundamental reasons, mostly because a majority of experienced dairy entrepreneurs were unwilling to share their secrets with the new entrants.

I found that aspiring dairy entrepreneurs were making similar mistakes that others had made when they started their enterprises.

There was no organized knowledge or mentorship that new entrants could draw upon to facilitate their journey and avoid the most common pitfalls. (They sought guidance from other unprofessional dairies, fabricators and other people who, because of their personal interest, hidden motives and unbaked knowledge, misguided them and caused them enormous losses)

Hence the journey of writing this book began so that I could bring out this information to all aspiring and struggling dairy entrepreneurs and enable them to succeed in their projects with zero failures.

With this intent to serve the dairy industry, I am bringing out a series of books and sharing all the information I have gathered over my years of experience and expertise to establish a successful and profitable dairy.

I did the required in-depth research and wrote this book to make people aware of the fundamentals of running a dairy enterprise, which otherwise leads to loss of time, money, energy and sometimes even the project's failure.

I promise that this book will empower dairy entrepreneurs with knowledge and insight that will save them from future losses.

Milk is widely consumed. It's a complete food and has a special place in the hearts of Indians. I am on a mission to help milk processing enterprises serve the entire society by providing good quality, healthy milk.

By doing this, I believe I am contributing in some way to my bigger goal of creating a healthy world around us.

Let's get Acquainted!

Hello, my name is Amardeep Singh Chadha, and I am a specialist in Dairy Equipment Engineering. Because of my intensive knowledge, deep understanding and extensive experience with the milk processing needs of the small-scale sector, people acknowledge me as an Expert in Dairy Entrepreneurship. I have a great passion for sharing my knowledge.

I am the Director at Chadha Sales Pvt. Ltd. (Dairy Equipment Engineers). Academically, I hold a Bachelor's degree in Commerce (B.Com) from Delhi University, a Post Graduate Diploma in Business Management from IILM Delhi, a Master's degree in Business Administration (MBA) from the European University, Belgium and a Diploma in Advance Computer Programming, from ICS Delhi.

I have enhanced my skills as a Certified Milking Machine Specialist from Denmark and have completed a Short-term Dairy course from KVK, NDRI, Karnal. I am also a Certified Manager by the German Federal Ministry of Economic Affairs & Energy.

In addition, I am an elected member of the "Central Executive Committee" of the Indian Dairy Association (IDA) 2022-2025. IDA works on the objective of **advancement of dairy science and industry, farming, animal husbandry, animal sciences and its branches, including dairy farming & research on breeding and management of dairy livestock.**

The family business of designing, manufacturing and marketing Dairy Equipment was set up by my grandfather, father and my uncle six decades ago, with a very humble beginning.

Today we have achieved new heights, growing multi-folds during the last two decades under my leadership, working along with my brothers. This growth and success, however, has not been a straight-line graph.

The growth has been marked with its own ups and downs, overcoming the numerous challenges & uncertainties that any and every entrepreneur faces.

I am also a founder of the Dairy Explorer Program, which is a framework to provide in-depth understanding and learning on key skills needed for running a successful milk processing business.

It is the platform on which I personally handhold the dairy entrepreneurs and be with them until they succeed in their ventures.

The reason for creating the Dairy Explorer platform was that many enthusiastic entrepreneurs want to invest in the Dairy sector but have limited knowledge. The lack of knowledge either results in the failure of the venture or the struggle to grow. The Dairy Explorer program provides in-depth knowledge about the various aspects of setting up successful Milk processing units.

Positive feedback in huge numbers proves that aspiring entrepreneurs found it extremely helpful in making decisions regarding entering the Dairy Business after learning through our Program.

The Explorer program is designed in a manner that, after attending it, even a layman/first timer can take a call, whether the setting up of a dairy falls under their ambit and whether they should go ahead with it or not. And also provides further deeper learning to existing dairy enterprises. It is a very comprehensive and to-the-point program.

It is a kind of reality check that needs to be done when one is ready to take a plunge. There are now around 337 plus Dairy Explorer Graduates who have taken this program and are thriving on their journey towards their dream dairy venture.

Today, I have reached a stage where I am in a position to help entrepreneurs in setting up successful and profitable Mini-dairy milk processing plant.

I have worked with more than 250 dairy entrepreneurs during the last two decades. I love to work with this closed group of entrepreneurs with passion and help them increase their income from the Dairy Business.

I have learned that to succeed in this sector, what you need most are the right kinds of guidance, directions and encouragement from successful entrepreneurs who have "been there and done that!"

There is a definite need for Guidance from successful entrepreneurs who have learnt from their mistakes so that new entrepreneurs need not repeat the same.

Take the classic example of the wheel. The wheel is already invented, and the new entrepreneurs just have to use the available knowledge and do not need to experiment all over again.

Similarly, there is a definite need to make a blueprint for establishing and operating a successful dairy business which the new entrepreneurs can use and thereby avoid all the mistakes made by their peers and be prepared to face the business challenges.

And this is exactly what I will be sharing with you, candidly and sincerely, in this publication - the secrets of successful enterprises who try to maintain secrecy because of fear of creating competition. I believe such knowledge is crucial for setting up a successful dairy business and must be shared to create healthy competition.

I will share with you in detail:

- How the dairy business works versus how it appears to work.

- Challenges and bottlenecks faced in setting up & operating a successful dairy processing unit, and

- Key functional areas which are basics for a successful mini dairy and dairy entrepreneurs must work upon.

This book has been written with the specific intention of supporting startup entrepreneurs who want to be successful and profitable in setting up milk processing units. However, it will also prove useful for ambitious dairies who would like to expand their business through vertical integration.

I also would like to mention explicitly that this book is not a dairy technology book. This book is written to apprise the upcoming, new or existing dairy units about what it takes to run a successful dairy enterprise.

I am on a mission to serve this sector by creating 10000 Successful entrepreneurs in the dairy Sector.

You could be next...

Wishing you overflowing success and profitability

Yours sincerely

Amardeep Singh Chadha

Navigating the Dynamic Flow of the Dairy Business!

We are in the era of ideas and startups. A lot of new entrepreneurs are coming up with many new ideas, new businesses and new ventures. When starting out, their intent is to set up a business that has the potential to provide them with a steady source of income.

So let's take a look at how an entrepreneur looking to set up a new business would normally generate ideas.

This is what they are most likely to do:

- Look around

- Talk to experts

- Discuss with peers

- Study and analyze various ideas

- Perform a SWOT analysis

- Shortlist options

- Finally, make a decision.

Taking this further, let's look at the factors that are likely to help them decide.

We can list the factors as under:

- Past performance

- Expert opinions

- Least affected by seasonal variations

- Price inelastic

- Always on the growth path

- High potential

More often than not, when entrepreneurs are looking to start up a new business, they gravitate toward the food business. Any essential food business is typically price inelastic, meaning its demand is least affected by price variations and has a rising demand with population growth.

However, there are many factors one has to consider while setting up a food business. Some of them are:

- Procurement of the right kind of ingredients

- Hiring of specialized staff

- Selection of the site & location

- Setting up the processing parameters suiting the customers' requirements, tastes, preferences, and so on.

So it isn't all that easy to venture into. Hence their next best bet appears to be the dairy industry.

It is a known fact that the milk & dairy business is one which is least affected by price and season. If we look at the milk production data, there is no question of price elasticity, and with the growing population and increase in per capita milk consumption, this figure is going up.

Moreover, every family needs milk and milk products in their diet. **Even during the pandemic, while the non-food businesses came to a close, milk being an essential commodity, the dairy industry was permitted to operate.**

Does this imply that the dairy business always succeeds?

No, it is a big NO!!! It is not always so!

This answer brings us to a very big question.

So, what **factors and issues should one consider before venturing into this sector and succeeding?**

These are multifold. The most important being that **milk is highly perishable and subject to a lot of adulteration.**

In addition, failure to select the right kind of raw material, the right kind of processing and the right distribution practices can all lead to failure.

We shall discuss these dynamics thoroughly and in detail in the following chapters.

The dairy business, although it appears straightforward and simple as well as easy to run and manage, comes with its fair share of problems.

Most of the time, the general understanding of the dairy business is a very simplistic one. Most people believe it is only the collection of milk from villagers or contractors and then packing and distributing it. And bang, you are in the dairy business.

That, my friends, however, is a dream. If this is what you think the dairy enterprise is all about and this is the mindset with which you are taking a holy dip in the dairy business, you are in for quite a surprise (maybe a rude shock even).

You are merely seeing the creamy layer on the top and are not aware of what goes into that flowy white fluid called milk. Beneath the visible calm of the rich & creamy layer, when you venture in-depth, there are plenty of ripples.

There are two ways in which you can be introduced to these ripple challenges:

1. Either as a shock, after taking the dip with your head totally down under.

2. Or as ready-to-navigate the ripples, riptides and whirlpools armed with advice & guidance from experts in the industry before making the decision to dive in.

As somebody who has been in this business for numerous years and has worked through a myriad of situations, let me give you the right perspective on the dairy business.

There is a famous statement by Ben Horowitz that says that **"Business ends up being very dynamic and situational."**

While this statement is true for almost any business, **it is especially apt for the dairy business.**

Aspiring entrepreneurs think that the dairy business is straightforward. However, instead of being straightforward and simple, the dairy business is extremely dynamic and situational, fraught with new operational challenges almost on a daily basis.

Dynamics change with the season, from place to place, with market interventions by big players, with the change in government policies, and so on.

This basically means that there is no single business plan or solution that fits all, or a formula or a trick which an entrepreneur can adapt to set up a successful and profitable milk processing business that would work successfully at all locations or anywhere in India and under all circumstances.

This business is so fluid (pun unintended) and dynamic that there are innumerable ways of doing it.

It all depends on who you are and, what your goal is, what it is that you want to do. So you need to find your own solutions, solve your own mysteries, and create your own journey to a successful and profitable dairy enterprise.

It is also to be understood that whenever we say "dairy", this could mean different things for different people. Dairy basically has three verticals.

- Number one is **"Milk Production"**- Anyone owning milk cattle, irrespective of the numbers, having a dairy farm and selling milk is called a "Dairy."

- The second vertical of dairy is **"Milk Processing"**, a unit or organization involved with any kind of treatment of raw milk to make it marketable, be it cooling or heating or cream separation or any other; the unit is also referred to as a "Dairy."

- The Third vertical is called "Milk Distribution" The person or the company in the business of buying and selling milk, transporting or in the business of logistics is also in the "Dairy" business, although they may not own any milk production or processing facility.

We can say that there is a **Dairy Farmer, a Dairy Processor and a Dairy Distributor** in the business of dairying.

What would you like to be?

You can take the role of either one or two or all three.

Dairy is a flourishing business, but there is no fixed template to set up the business. Having worked across many areas of the country, I can guarantee you that the solution that works in Uttaranchal cannot be blindly applied to Hyderabad, or what works for the Hyderabad region cannot be replicated in different parts of the same state. Milk production, milk pricing and consumption patterns throughout the country, state-wise and region-wise, are not fixed or constant. They always vary.

That is how dynamic, situational and area-specific the dairy business is.

With India being the largest producer of milk in the world, the opportunities in this sector are tremendous. It is a complex but profitable business, but only if you know how to navigate the complexities and the flow of the business. It is these challenges and the secrets to successfully overcoming these challenges that I will be sharing with you in detail in the coming chapters.

Sourcing it Right

"Quality is important. Watery milk will give leaking profits. But quality must not be overpaid for. Striking the right balance between quality and price while procuring milk is the key to success in the dairy business."

~Amardeep Singh Chadha

Sourcing is the first and most critical decision one needs to take. The most important factor for the dairy industry or any other manufacturing industry is the availability and sourcing of raw materials. **And for dairy, it is the one and only 'White Gold', the complete food 'Milk'.**

Sourcing the milk at the right time, at the right price, at the right place, in the right quantity and most importantly, of the right quality is the key to a successful dairy business. It can make or break it.

Sourcing is a composite of 3 important factors that include:

- What to source?
- Where to source from?

- At what price to source?

Let's explore these components in detail one by one.

What to source?

When we talk about what to source, it defines the quality of milk, **be it organoleptic quality, chemical quality or bacteriological quality.**

The quality has to be defined as per the needs of the entrepreneur and what products and processing have to be done.

For example, if, as an entrepreneur, you intend to go in for raw milk chilling and sale, you must focus on sourcing the best organoleptic quality. Or for pasteurized, sterilized or UHT milk, its protein stability is important, and so on. Therefore your end goal will define the qualitiy/s you need to keep in mind while sourcing your raw material.

From where to source?

There are various sources and various places where you could go around to source milk. The most obvious place to start would be areas near your location where milk could be available.

It is important to understand that there are primarily three options from whom milk could become available to you:

- One would be the **organized dairy farmers** who can supply milk to you.

- Second would be the **semi-organized dairy farmers,** and

- The third is the **homegrown farmers.**

Organized Dairy Farms

To have more clarity on the subject, let's first understand organised dairy farms. Organised dairy farms are the ones which have been set up as per the animal husbandry practices, and they have a large number of cattle, say anywhere between 40 to 400 Plus. Dairy Farming is the primary business for them.

Semi-organized Dairy Farms

Semi-organized farms are those farms which are basically located on the outskirts of cities, and their formation is in clusters. Typically, these farms have 5 to 40 milch animals and prefer to sell their milk directly to the customers in these cities. In a milk shed area, there may be a number of such clusters.

Homegrown Dairy Farmers

Lastly, homegrown farmers are the ones who live in the villages and own one or two milking animals for their families only. After the consumption by the family, the remaining leftover milk, called a marketable surplus, is sold to the dairies, milk chilling centers, milk processors, and milk contractors to supplement their household income.

These farmers may either supply the milk to the village-level co-operative milk societies or the collection centers set up in their villages by the milk processors, or even, in many cases, the buyers may come to their doorsteps and collect the surplus milk.

The Dairy processor has to make the decision of sourcing milk best suited to their circumstances, location and logistics.

Of the total milk production of India, approximately 10% of the milk is produced by organized dairy farms, 20% by semi-organized farmers and 70% of the milk produced in India is contributed by homegrown farmers.

India is one of the largest producers of milk in the world. From the above statistics, it is understood that India is number one because milk production is majorly contributed by homegrown farmers.

Undoubtedly, it is the growth of homegrown farmers which has contributed to India being numero uno in the world milk production.

While they are the ones on whom milk processors can depend for the milk quality, we have to consider the logistics of collecting milk from a large number of homegrown farmers, as the surplus available with each may not be in large quantities.

The organized dairy farms' milk is also offered to milk processors. They also prefer to sell their milk at a premium, either as raw fresh, raw chilled or pasteurized & packed by setting up an integrated dairy farm.

An integrated dairy farm means a farm with its own dairy processing capabilities. They process their own milk and supply it to the consumer directly, getting good value for the milk.

Hence procurement of milk from organized milk farmers would be expensive although, logistically, it provides a better choice, as the milk can be collected from a single source. However, dependence on a single source is fraught with a huge risk.

Unlike any other agricultural produce, milk has to be produced daily, collected daily, processed daily and delivered daily. Any failure on the part of the supplier, for whatever reason, shall adversely affect the dairy processor dependent on them for milk procurement.

By the same logic, the semi-organized farms, which are located on the outskirts of towns, selling the milk directly to the consumers, are not the ones on which small milk processors can depend for obvious reasons.

The homegrown farmers who actually feed the animals from their own produce, use their household labor and sell the surplus milk after meeting their family needs may be the best options for the new entrepreneurs setting up milk processing plants as the milk production cost would be lowest by homegrown farmers, **hence targeting them as the milk vendors for the dairies shall not only provide good quality milk but also at the lowest price on which one can set up a successful and profitable dairy business.**

Lastly, at what price to source?

Price will always make or break the business.

Of course, there are other issues in the milk pricing -

- Whether to buy per liter basis
- Or total solids basis
- Or fat basis

- Or on a two-axis pricing basis.

- Should there be a minimum and maximum Fat & SNF or total solids level which shall form the basis for accepting or rejecting milk?

- Should there be any bonus or penalty?

So there is no one formula to calculate the buying price of the milk as it could be different for different states or even district-wise.

Dairy Cooperatives would calculate in a different manner, and private dairies are likely to calculate in different ways. However, an entrepreneur should understand the complexities of price calculation in the area where they would source the milk.

The best way to purchase milk is on a two-axis pricing basis.

These are some of the decisions an entrepreneur has to take, and all the details affecting these decisions should be well understood by the entrepreneurs.

Possibilities of Growth in the Dairy Industry

The Government of India, in association with the Department of Animal Husbandry and Dairying, in June 2020 announced a $ 2.1 Billion infrastructure development fund with an interest subsidy scheme to promote investment by private players and MSMEs in the dairy industry, meat processing and animal feed plants.

The opportunities are tremendous!

To understand this effectively, it would be better if you are aware of and understand the origin, history and development of the dairy industry.

The history of dairy in the Indian subcontinent goes back roughly 8,000 years to the first domestication of zebu cattle, which is thought to have originated in India.

By the beginning of the Indus Valley civilization, zebu cattle had been fully domesticated and used for their milk. In the Vedic period, milk was one of the primary elements of the typical diet. Milk, curds, and ghee were important elements of food in the Indian subcontinent over the reigns of rulers from different religious backgrounds.

Dairy in India was once a largely subsistence-oriented occupation intended to produce milk for home consumption. In 1919, a dairy animal census was conducted for the first time by British colonial officials. A report authored in 1937 indicated a sub-optimal rate of milk consumption in the country. **It estimated a per capita intake of 7 ounces (200 g) per day (inclusive of all dairy products), which was the lowest among all large dairy countries.**

In the 1920s, modern milk processing and marketing technologies were introduced in India. The National Dairy Development Board (NDDB) was founded in 1965. It launched Operation Flood in 1969–70, a program aimed at modernizing and developing the dairy sector using a model to set up Dairy co-operatives.

During this period, dairy cooperatives emerged as a dominant force based on the "Anand Model". This model evolved in Anand, Gujarat, having begun there in 1946, and came to be adopted all over the country.

Operation Flood proceeded in three phases. Phase I (1970–1981), Phase II (beginning 1986), and Phase III, which continued to the mid-1990s, expanded investment still further to a number of smaller towns.

Since 1997, India has become the world's largest Milk producer, when it surpassed the United States. At present,

India has the highest level of Milk production and consumption of all countries the world over.

Dairy is the single largest agricultural commodity contributing 5 per cent of the national economy and employing more than 8 crore farmers directly. India is ranked 1st in milk production, contributing 23 per cent of global milk production. Milk production in the country has grown at a compound annual growth rate of about 6.2 per cent to reach 209.96 million tons in 2020-21 from 146.31 million tons in 2014-15 (Source: Economic Survey, 2021-22).

Today, India is largely self-sufficient in milk production. Milk production in India increased approximately Eightfold between 1968 and 2021.

Another important inference is that of the total milk production of 190 million tons, only 52.6 mnt or **27.7% is procured by the organized dairy industry,** and out of which 30 mnt is used for the liquid milk balance, 22.6 mnt goes into products like curd, ghee, chhena, paneer etc.

Now, We know about the huge potential in the dairy sector, in terms of the availability of milk as surplus and the gap in the market which can be picked, currently being sourced by traditional or unorganized sectors.

Now the point is that as India is growing, it is developing super fast, and we will soon be a developed country. Similarly, this 27% organized player share will increase, and whoever has taken the position in the organized sector in India will grow exponentially with the growth of the dairy industry, which is expected to increase by 9-11 per cent in 2021-22, driven by a revival in economic activities, increasing per capita consumption of milk and milk products, according to a report.

If we look at the developed nations, their organized market share varies from approximately 80% to 95%. This shows the huge potential to go up from the current 27%. In absolute terms, even if we double the milk handling by the organized sector, this shall imply setting up another 55-60 mnt processing capacity which translates to a per day capacity of 13-14 crores liters.

That is a huge figure by any standards and would be benefited by dairy enterprises that will be part of the race to expand or grow.

The Government of India, on its part, is playing a big role and has given a big boost to the dairy industry with budgetary support as well as in the form of subsidies for setting up the cold chain, processing of milk and setting up of milk processing units.

On the regulatory front also, food regulations and regulatory bodies in India have been active for more than a decade now.

Food Safety and Standards Authority of India (FSSAI), a statutory body established by the Ministry of Health & Family Welfare, Government of India, under the Food Safety and Standards Act, 2006, has been formed, and a lot of activities are going on in India to safeguard and control the quality of food and milk. Therefore this more stringent implementation of the Food Safety and Standards Act in India will lead to more growth of the organized players in the dairy industry.

So the milk industry will definitely take a major leap in its journey from 27% to 80% in the organized sector.

Are you ready to take up your place and profitability in this fast-growing sector?

In 2018–19, the per capita availability of milk in India was 394 grams per day. India's per capita availability of milk was 427 grams per day in 2020-21 (provisional).

If we look further from the consumption point of view, the per capita liquid milk consumption in India on average is approximately 60 Kg/year vis-a-vis the highest being 115 Kg in Belarus (Data of 2021)

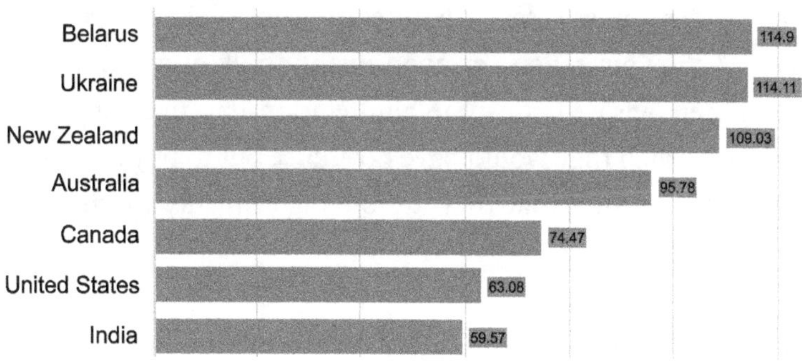

Graph: Global per capita Consumption of fluid milk 2021, published by Statista Research Department July 27, 2022.

Hence there is a vast potential if we have to double up the liquid milk consumption to the level of Belarus. And if we look at the total milk consumption, including products, it is a whopping 431 Kg per annum in Finland and merely 85 Kg in India.

As I said earlier, the potential to set up new units is vast, and that is when we know that milk production in the country is on the growth path. By the year 2050, India's share in the world milk production is expected to be 45% which is currently at 23%.

Doubling the milk production means the gap between the organized and unorganized shall further increase if new units are not set up, and milk & milk production in the country does not increase to the level of the developed nations.

While India is the largest producer of milk, it is also the place where most cases of adulteration in milk have come to light. As the awareness for good quality milk grows and more consumers wish to consume adulteration-free milk and milk products, then they would have no choice but to buy a branded product to ensure that they are buying a quality product.

Again to emphasize:

- There is a huge gap in milk production and milk being handled by the organized sector. 75% of the total milk is handled by the unorganized sector.
- Per capita consumption of fluid milk, as well as milk & milk products in the country, is very low.

- And milk production in the country is on a growth path, and almost half the milk in the world shall be produced in the country by 2050. Provides potential for export also.

All that I have shared in this chapter should be enough evidence to understand that there will certainly be no dearth of growth in the dairy Sector.

Benefits of a Mini Dairy

In the preceding pages, we learnt about the tremendous growth potential existing in the dairy industry.

Setting up a mini dairy to process wholesome quality milk appears to be a very lucrative business proposal. But the mute question is, why a mini dairy?

If the potential is so big, why not a large milk processing plant with multi products processing? It is obvious that the larger the quantity of milk processed, the higher shall be the turnover and, thus, the higher the prospects of earning more.

But if we consider the total scenario, a larger plant means higher investment and bigger infrastructure, whether it be the procurement of milk or milk processing or milk marketing.

For a new entrant, it is always beneficial to go for a mini dairy unless, of course, it is for a corporation which already has all the resources at its disposal and will have merit in going on a big scale.

So what are the benefits which an entrepreneur will derive by setting up a mini dairy over a medium size or large-scale unit?

Template to expand: It is best to begin the journey as a pilot project to learn the basics of any business and especially so in the dairy industry, as milk is highly perishable, and the fact has been emphasized a number of times.

Any wrong decision shall result in the spoilage of milk and money going down the drain. It is not important how big a dairy we go for; rather, it is important whatever size of dairy we go for, it should be profitable and successful. Hence, an entrepreneur can start small, and once they understand the business, they can scale up fast.

Control on Milk procurement

As emphasized in the earlier chapter, it is of utmost importance to understand that the basis of a successful and profitable manufacturing venture is the procurement of raw materials. In this case, it is **"The Milk"**. It will be easier for a mini dairy to set up its milk procurement system as it will depend on a smaller number of milk producers or farmers. Slowly, by building confidence and making lifelong relationships with the farmers, it will be able to build up to bigger things in future.

Access to Quality Milk

Bad-quality milk produces poor-quality products leading to the failure of the enterprise. Undoubtedly, a mini dairy would have an advantage over others in **access to quality Milk.**

Milk is highly perishable because it is an excellent medium for the growth of microorganisms–particularly bacterial pathogens – that can cause spoilage. So the quickest and nearest collection is the best option for sourcing and preserving quality milk.

Procurement of milk for a mini dairy shall be region limited, which means timely and nearby collection and timely preservation of the quality by cooling it and then processing it soonest.

A mini dairy requiring a low quantity of milk finds it easier to source the milk from the neighbourhood and thus have access to collecting quality milk.

Delivery in the Shortest Period

Another advantage the mini dairy has is in terms of logistics. A shorter product chain is indicative of a much simpler ecosystem.

We don't realise how much milk has to travel to reach consumers' homes. When milk is produced in a nearby region, there is less use of fuel which is a good option for the environment and can deliver the milk from the farm to the consumer's table in the shortest possible time. In contrast, in many cases, the big plants may take a week or even more.

Hence the freshness of milk is ensured when one gets it from a mini dairy.

Not to forget that being vocal about where you produce or collect the milk and how you transport your goods can get you a long way with consumers.

Regional Advantage

A mini dairy would always be a regional player, at least to start with and would give you lots of **local advantages.**

As encouraged by our Prime Minister, Shri Narendra Modi, being **"Vocal for Local" has urged more people to buy local products.**

With a mini dairy, you would have the advantage of being recognised as a regional player who collects fresh & delivers fresh.

Being a regional player develops strong social bonds in the local communities, and mini-dairies take advantage of regional players.

If local production grows, we are directly creating new jobs, sources of income and economic development. In the long run, this will mean a bigger local market, which will brighten the future of local homegrown producers. This is beneficial for both local producers and local consumers and, of course, for mini dairy enterprises.

Lower Processing & Operational Costs

If the mini dairies are operated at optimum capacity, they are mostly in an advantageous position as they would have lower processing and lower operational costs. This is because:

- The operations of mini dairies are flexible and can increase or decrease the output as per the market demands by increasing or decreasing the hours of operations.

- Mini dairies have flexibility in their operations as they can easily shift from one product to another with minimum effort and without adding any additional capital equipment. For example, the multi-purpose kettle can be used to heat the milk for making curd/fermented products, to manufacture paneer/coagulated products or even for manufacturing mawa or ghee.

- The advantages in operational cost coupled with better control of the quality of raw milk procured lead to better end products, giving them price advantages and thereby increased margins.

Fetch Higher Prices

Mini dairies have a dedicated customer base in their area who have the power and willingness to pay for the quality, and thus mini dairies are in a position to **fetch higher prices.**

A mini dairy can also get better prices as it can create and modify its product specifications according to the taste and demand of the local consumers, which a larger dairy would not be able to do easily because it would produce according to its large customer base.

To sell milk and milk products at a premium, one needs to have an effective marketing strategy with a unique selling proposition for each offering.

A lot of customers in India look for fresh dairy products; hence the regional player is preferred, and in turn, mini dairies can fetch better prices in the market.

Higher Margins and Shorter Payback Period

When we talk about profitability, if you compare with various other businesses, you will find that dairy businesses have **higher margins and shorter payback periods**, which could vary from an ROI of 3% to 6%.

A detailed project report will give you the nearest idea of the profitability of your project, which ideally should be created and by analyzing the numbers, you could verify the returns your project will give.

It is enough to understand that the dairy industry is one wherein one can have a multifold turnover of the capital invested and always has shorter payback periods.

For example, with an investment of 100 Lakhs working capital, one can have a turnover of 700 to 1000 Lakhs per annum. No other industry can have such lucrative return figures.

Flexibility in Operations

Lastly, a very important point is that dairy businesses have flexibility in operations.

Generally, any business which is rigid and cannot be changed becomes inefficient over a time period and has difficulty in growth. Many times there are responses to be made in the market, and if the business responds with their action faster, the business builds sustainability.

Mini dairy's operations are such that they can give a quick response to the market, triggers and shifts. Hence sustainability is higher due to flexibility in operations.

Challenges
in Setting up a Mini Dairy

Earlier in the book, we learnt about the benefits mini dairy processors have over medium and large-sized plants before they themselves go large.

In the process of overcoming the pitfalls and reaping the benefits, there will likely be a number of challenges which an entrepreneur will have to face.

Let us take a look at these challenges and understand them better in order to overcome or bypass them:

1. Milk Availability:

The first challenge on the list is Milk Availability. It may appear ridiculous that if we are the largest milk producer in the world, why is milk availability a challenge?

Let me clarify that milk availability per se isn't a challenge. However, sourcing the right quality of milk at the right place, in the right quantity and at the right price is a challenge which has to be overcome.

By availability, we refer to the marketable surplus, non-availability due to competition with unorganized players, seasonal variations, milk availability at far-off places, and so on.

By milk availability, I also mean that there is a lean season when milk production is less, and then there is the flush season when milk production is higher.

This means the supply of milk will fluctuate as per the season, and we would never get the same amount of milk all year long in our collection system.

Whereas consumer demand for milk will remain constant around the year. Now a mini dairy entrepreneur would have to face a challenge in maintaining a balance between supply and demand to fulfil the needs of consumers.

2. Competing with Established brands

The second challenge is there are already established brands in the market. These brands have established themselves in a relatively short time period. In the past 15-20 years, even the small dairies have become so huge that they are established nationwide and have a complete network for sales and distribution.

Now when a small dairy or a mini dairy enters the market with its product, they have to compete with established big brands, which is a very challenging task.

The bigger dairie's marketing budgets are huge, whereas small dairies cannot even think of having their own marketing set-up.

Also, the distribution network of established players and their relationship with dealers & distributors is so strong that they influence them to push back the new brands so much that they do not even get placed on the retail shelves.

Hence mini dairy entrepreneurs have to learn marketing skills by which they can grab a decent market share, or they can take another route where they do not compete; instead, they go for niche marketing.

3. Brand Loyalty

The third challenge comes at the consumer level, that is, "Brand Loyalty".

Imagine a consumer who has been buying and using a particular brand for a long time, and then suddenly, a new brand comes into the market advertising and claiming it is the best brand, with superb quality.

Still, people **won't** buy that brand easily. They will give different reasons if asked, like,

- "I have been buying this existing brand for long, and I am completely satisfied with it",

- "The existing brand suits me in every way, so I don't feel like changing it." or

- "Our taste buds are settled to this brand, and we don't want to change" and so on.

The customer is resistant to change to the new brands. This is very disheartening and de-motivating for a new dairy to see intransigence, rigid choices and viewpoints about the brand.

Though this is an unavoidable challenge, one can combat it through marketing skills by creating a strong and unique selling proposition or with attractive brand promises.

4. Procurement Competition

Procurement competition means competition in milk collection.

Generally, in all businesses, you will find there exists competition in marketing and there is competition in selling, but the dairy business is a unique business which has competition not only in the market but also in procurement, that is, in buying raw materials also.

Normally if you go to any business, you will find there is competition in the market but getting raw materials is very easy when you start some other business.

In fact, a lot of raw material suppliers will come to you and say buy my material, but in dairy, it does not happen that way because whoever is producing milk is already having a tie-up with existing processors.

As a new person, when you go for collection and say I want milk, then you have to offer them something better to get milk from them. This influencing factor could be price; it could be your services, it could be your position, it could be your reputation in the market etc. Since getting milk from the collection is imperative, milk procurement competition is a very real challenge in this dairy industry.

5. Working Capital Management

Another challenge in the dairy business is **Working Capital Management.** The dairy business is a cash business. I have seen that a lot of dairy businesses struggle to grow because they are not capable of managing their working capital.

Let us understand it better through an example: if we buy milk on credit for 10 days and have to give credit to our customers for 30 days, then 20 days of working capital should be available in our pocket; otherwise, we can't grow.

So Working Capital Management is also one of the challenges in this dairy industry, especially when we need to grow our dairy faster.

6. Perishable Nature of Milk

The last challenge is one that probably everyone knows milk is a **perishable** product. If we do not take care of the milk in the right manner, using the right technology, with the right technique and through the right process, then it will result in sour and spoiled milk. This will simply mean a huge loss to us. So, even small negligences and improper handling of the milk can cause significant losses in this business.

These are the myriad challenges that any new entrant to the industry is likely to face.

Now that you are aware of these challenges, it will be easy for you to prepare yourself and avoid these pitfalls.

Why do Dairies Fail in India?

It is quite well known that a lot of new dairies are being set up in India, and a lot of them close down or struggle to grow due to one reason or another.

As per research data released by the Bureau of Labor Statistics, Nearly 20 per cent of small businesses fail within the first year.

30 per cent of businesses are likely to fail by the end of the second year.

Approximately half will have failed by the end of the fifth year.

And only 30 per cent of businesses will remain by the end of the decade — a 70 per cent failure rate.

Here let's pause for a moment and review some important facts that we have established by now:

- India is the largest milk producer in the world; there is no shortage of raw milk,
- labour is available in plenty,

- After China, our nation is the second most populated country in the world. This makes India a vast potential market. The Mckinsey Global Institute predicts that by **2025, 69 cities** individually are likely to have a population of 1 million each individually.

- There is no shortage of infrastructure or capital.

- Technology and engineering are easily available

The bonus is **India's improved ranking under the World Bank's parameters of the "Ease of Doing Business", which proves that there is a conducive environment for venturing into and then succeeding at new businesses.**

But still, when new dairy processing units are set up, a large number of them fail.

Why? Why do they fail? What are the pitfalls?

There could be several reasons for the same, and here I am introducing you to the most common ones so that you can learn to side-step them on your way to success:

Sourcing of Milk

To start with, there is high competition for milk procurement among the various players, and mini-dairies often get overpowered by the other players, failing to get the right quality of milk at the right price. Often you will be faced with difficulty in sourcing the right kind of milk according to the end product you have to make. It is important to source the right composition of milk with respect to the product we intend to make so that we can achieve the desired product quality. **Not finding the same can cause businesses to fail.**

Government Policy

In some states like Karnataka, Rajasthan, Jharkhand, & Telangana, State Governments provide subsidies to dairy farmers per litre of milk, which they supply to state dairy cooperatives. And more often than not, private dairies are expected to match these subsidized prices. Hence there is a high cost of milk collection, and they struggle to grow.

For example, Karnataka Govt gives Rs. 5/- per litre to Karnataka Milk Federation milk producers for milk having min of 3.5% Fat and 8.5% SNF. So the milk producer members and non-members of the cooperative would have different privileges.

Competition & lack of infrastructure

State Dairy Cooperatives get Substantial aid from NDDB, the Central Government, and the World Bank for many years for developing infrastructure. With these aids, they have built huge infrastructures making other companies unable to match the volumes.

Thus we can safely say that competition with the Cooperative sector is a hassle for the growth of mini dairies.

Supply Chain Logistics

It is a heck of a task to establish the supply chain for milk collection. Logistics is the highest cost in the cost structure of milk. So a lot of mini dairies struggle due to high logistics costs. And due to this higher logistics cost, they are not able to either start up or sustain their enterprise. The cost of collection per litre of milk becomes very high if the collection is of a small quantity.

Seasonal Variations

Due to seasonal variation in milk production, during the lean season, the cost of collection per litre of milk tends to go up, and it shoots up pretty high.

Selection of the Wrong Product Mix

Having the right product mix is critical to the success of a dairy. You need to be sensitive to the consumer's needs. There are numerous decisions to be made — Whether to go for double-toned milk and butter/ghee (from surplus fat)? Or full cream milk? To go for consumer packs or bulk packs? Or khoa or paneer or curd? If milk remains unsold, what to do? These are the questions which entrepreneurs fail to address before jumping in. Hence struggle and Failures.

Unprofessional Business Plan

The next very common yet critical pitfall, especially for new start-ups, is that dairies choose the wrong strategies.

By strategy, I mean that start-ups create a weak business plan which should ideally be thoroughly worked upon before putting any money into the business. In the business world, we say that 80% of our efforts should go into planning, and the balance 20% should go into execution. Whereas a lot of young entrepreneurs straight away jump to the execution part, and obviously, they get unexpected results and are in for a rough journey.

Over Focus on Equipment

A lot of new small companies that come into this dairy sector think that just by buying the machines and equipment, they will be able to run their dairy enterprise successfully.

That is a myth.

We have many examples of companies which invested in the best plant and machinery but were still not able to reach the ladder of success. So a lot of dairies struggle or fail as they just concentrate on buying machinery and equipment and ignore all the other factors they need to take care of.

Copying other Dairies

A lot of new entrepreneurs look at successful dairies as to what and how they are executing and their way of doing things, and they just start copying the dairy that they admire.

But now you are aware that the dairy business ends up being dynamic and situational. So I am sure you will understand that copying other dairies will not be the success path as your market and situation would be different from theirs.

Instead, you will need to invent and figure out your original way of getting into the dairy market.

Selection of Poor Technology

A lot of new dairy entrepreneurs fall into the sweet trap of cheap machinery suppliers. Due to that, there are constant breakdowns and the outcome of product quality is not achieved. A machinery supplier should not be responsible for the equipment only; a good supplier would be responsible for the output you receive from it.

Inefficient Operations

Efficiency in operations help to reduce the processing costs, get better recovery from the milk, increase efficiency, reduce costs, increase output, increase productivity, control wastage, more savings etc. and hence make the dairies profitable. Failure to adopt efficient technology or use energy-efficient equipment causes the downfall of dairies.

Lack of Knowledge

Irrespective of the industry, to be successful, there is always a need to upgrade one's knowledge about the processes, testing techniques, better product manufacturing methods and so on. However, many entrepreneurs fail to keep up with the current knowledge. Shockingly, many do not even acquire the basic knowledge and just jump in. Both these scenarios spell downfall.

Success Secrets: The Four Pillars of Profitable Dairies

In the last chapter, we talked about the reasons for the struggles and challenges that dairy enterprises face and go through as well as the different causes for the failure of dairy enterprises.

Now that you are thoroughly aware of all the pitfalls, **it is important to understand those factors which are the foundation of creating a successful and profitable dairy.**

As such, there could be many areas which will help to create success which includes your leadership, the vision of the enterprise, developing a good business strategy, managing products as well as services, selling skills, financial management, good service with deliveries and so on...

But if we focus on the aspects of the dairy business and look at dairy companies that have shown growth, have a stronger base in the market and are difficult for any competitor to beat, We will find some factors that are common in their success.

Irrespective of the size of the dairy, if we consolidate the learnings from all these companies, it has been found that there are four common areas that function as the pillars of a successful and profitable dairy processing business.

Let us first understand why we are talking about the Pillars.

Are we all not aware that any civil building that has a strong foundation and sturdy Pillars can withstand adversities, be it quakes, storms or floods? The building will continue to stay tall.

But if the pillars are weak, the vagaries of weather shall be enough to cause them to fall down over the years.

In the same way, a business set up with a strong foundation and on sturdy pillars shall survive the competition despite bad times, hefty challenges or arduous struggles to come out successfully.

Without further ado, let's understand one by one what these pillars of a successful dairy business are...

Pillar No.1: Milk Quality Control

Natural State of Milk

The most critical marker of milk quality is its comparison to the nearest natural condition of milk, and if, in comparison, it does not qualify the same as a natural product, it would be considered poor quality.

So we can say the quality of milk refers to its degree of the natural state. Milk has distinctive chemical characteristics or attributes. The natural quality of milk depends upon the species of the animal, breed of the animal, feed given to the animal etc.

So, successful dairy enterprises must know how they can keep their milk quality to the nearest natural state.

Good-quality raw milk has to be free of the following:

- extraneous matter & sediment
- off-flavours
- abnormal colour
- Abnormal odour
- low in bacterial count
- free of chemicals
- free of antibiotics
- abnormal acidity

The quality of raw milk is the primary factor determining the quality of milk products. Good-quality milk products can be produced only from good-quality raw milk.

All new entrepreneurs seeking success in the dairy sector must be aware of the different aspects of milk quality. It is important to understand that just as it's impossible to reverse our age similarly, once the milk deteriorates, it can not be reversed, or the quality cannot be improved upon.

We only can control the quality of milk where it stands. So you can only control the quality and not build it.

Understanding the milk and milk components and what leads to its spoilage is very important.

Milk is the most perishable commodity, and maintaining its quality as it comes out of the udder of the animals requires proper care, handling and earliest possible preservation (by cooling it) or processing before it deteriorates.

Good Milk, Bad Milk, Standard and Substandard Milk

A dairy entrepreneur should be able to distinguish between Good Milk, Bad Milk, and Standard and Substandard Milk.

Here you also need to understand that, strange though it may sound, Good Milk can also be Substandard Milk, and Bad Milk could also be Standard Milk.

Let me explain how this could become possible.

Milk may be free of any extraneous matter, appear good, natural and have a sweet taste, but maybe the composition of milk is not as per FSSAI regulations, and hence it shall be Good milk but Substandard, not meeting the standards for Fat & SNF as prescribed by the FSSAI.

On the other hand, it may be of the highest standards for Fat & SNF and other parameters but not handled properly. It may have a high bacterial load, a short time left to sour and shall be considered poor quality.

Good dairy enterprises follow FSSAI instructions and try to abide by those. And mostly small and micro dairies do not even follow FSSAI norms. Instructions by FSSAI provide only the parameters, which are the maximum and minimum limits of various quality parameters of milk and milk products. A dairy entrepreneur should create their own intelligence, understanding, and wisdom to control the milk quality, which comes through understanding milk properties and composition and through case studies and practical training.

Adulteration

New dairy entrepreneurs are hesitant to step into the business as they fear that adulteration is part and parcel of the business, and they may not be able to identify or deal with it. They are fearful of being taken for a ride and, in the process tarnishing their reputation unknowingly.

However, this shouldn't deter you from entering a business that has a lot of growth opportunities and profit potential. Initially, you can avail of the services or guidance of an expert to identify and control adulteration and then, with time, you must ensure that you understand the ways and types of adulteration of milk to avoid them and control quality.

Milk Quality Assurance

Furthermore, a successful dairy entrepreneur should be apprised of the FSSAI standards, testing methods and apparatus and know the testing procedure so that in any adverse condition, they are capable of managing the milk quality control in their enterprise.

It is possible to control and maintain milk quality using the numerous available testing methods. This quality testing will ensure that the products are safe and healthy and they conform to the standards of purity, chemical composition and bacteria/microorganism levels.

Here is what a good quality control system does: it ensures that milk & milk products are of desired quality and then maintains that quality control through appropriate methods.

Having a good quality control system in place is crucial for dairies as it ensures that their consumers receive products of the highest possible quality and not contaminated or sub-standard products that could endanger their health.

Therefore it is critical to a dairy's success to ensure that its quality testing & control mechanisms conform to domestic as well as international standards of acceptability.

Like the saying 'Charity begins at home', similarly quality control begins right at the first step — meaning right at the source, the farm where the milk is produced.

Farmers must be sensitised to the importance of adhering to correct practices of milk production and handling milk. They must also be encouraged to ensure compliance with Government regulations regarding adulteration as well as the usage of veterinary drugs on cattle that are lactating.

To operate a successful dairy, all businesses should ensure thorough checking of all the milk collected from different sources before processing it. To ensure that the milk is safe and healthy, it needs to be checked chemically, organoleptically and bacteriologically.

Any abnormal smell or appearance in the milk collected is an indicator of bad milk. The common cause for this is advanced acidification.

Other than that, any milk tainted with chemicals or drugs or milk that comes from animals fed with malting residues will show discoloration and have a particular flavor and is a marker of bad milk.

In addition, other common causes of bad milk could be atmospheric or bacterial taints. Also, milk from animals in late lactation is likely to be spontaneously rancid.

Exposure to light and the presence of heavy metals due to any reason can also cause milk to go bad.

Another thing that dairy businesses need to keep in mind is that raw milk contains fat. However, in good-quality, fresh milk, this fat should always be a homogenous part of the milk, completely mixed with it. If the fat rises to the surface as globules forming a separate layer on top, you need to pay attention.

This could be because the milk was allowed to stand for some time, or it could be due to excessive agitation during transportation. Previous freezing and then thawing could also lead to the separation of fat, and another cause could be adulteration, as the sediments and particles of the adulteration material could show up separately.

All these quality issues can be identified and controlled by the practice of appropriate tests.

Organoleptic and COB (clot on boiling) tests right on the farm or at the collection center(s) are the key.

Certain other advanced tests to check density-specific gravity, fat content and adulteration etc., can only be performed at the collection centers or dairy laboratories. Chemical and bacteriological testing will also be possible at the collection centers and labs only.

We have already understood that good raw material (good-quality milk in this case) is critical to delivering high-grade products. Therefore the grading of milk to accept only good quality and reject bad milk is essential to successful dairy operations.

This can only be possible when the dairy entrepreneur is well versed in the testing methodologies, and they should be capable of identifying off-flavours and their causes.

They also need to be disciplined enough to make an effort to religiously check all the milk received from various sources.

Here I am sharing with you, in detail, the four major but simple quality tests that are enough to meet the quality control needs of mini dairies.

These Tests though simple, will ensure that you deliver only good quality milk if you use them properly and consistently.

The Organoleptic Test

This is one of the simplest yet most effective tests that involve only your sense of sight and smell.

Simple rule of thumb; if the milk looks or smells different (meaning abnormal) in any way or appears to have any foreign particles, it should be instantly rejected without thinking twice.

New dairy entrepreneurs often underestimate the importance and effectiveness of organoleptic testing. If they practice it even for 15 days consistently, they will develop a keen sense of color, taste and smell of good and bad milk and will become discerning experts at it.

Clot on Boiling (COB) Test

Another quick, simple and effective test is the Clot on boiling (COB). It helps in identifying the acidity level of milk, as high-acidity milk should be rejected because it can cause problems with boiling or being heated during processing.

The Alcohol Test

This test is more sensitive than the COB test. COB only detects milk which is highly acidic. It is capable of detecting even medium-acidity milk.

Milk Composition Test

The common problem is that milk producers indulge in the addition of water and other substances to milk to increase their profits. This can be easily tested with instruments, kits and analyzers. Therefore it is essential for dairies to be equipped with the appropriate instruments and kits to analyze the quality of milk.

By using these simple tools and tests, you can set up a quality control system that will prove to be a good starting point on your journey to success.

A successful and profitable enterprise should know how to implement a **Milk Quality Control System** using simple ways & means which ensure that the dairy handles only good-quality milk.

This improves the dairy entrepreneur's reputation as a quality milk supplier and ultimately increases its profits.

Pillar No.2: Procurement

Once the concept of milk quality is understood, the next step is to learn about the procurement of milk. In order to be successful, one needs to learn - what quality, how much quantity, from which source and at what price to procure milk.

Let me elaborate on these one by one...

Quality of milk

The quality of milk has already been explained thoroughly in detail in the previous chapter and also earlier in the book.

As explained earlier, I am doing a quick recap here. The quality of milk needs to be controlled in terms of

- Its organoleptic acceptability, that is, taste, smell, colour and appearance;

- Chemical quality in terms of fat content, SNF content, acidity, protein stability,

- Bacteriological quality (microorganisms per ml of milk)

- And the most important one is the milk being free of adulterants, neutralizers & chemical preservatives.

Quantity of milk

It is important to procure the optimum quantity of milk. **In the initial years, mini dairies tend to procure more milk than they can sell.** It is a well-known fact that milk is a highly perishable commodity, and it is produced daily and has to be collected every day.

In case any milk is left over, either it has to be disposed of at considerably lower prices or converted to products which are not bulky and can be stored for some time, even if there is no requirement or demand, or else it has to be somehow consumed.

Over-procurement of milk is one of the major reasons mini dairies struggle to grow. On the other hand, procuring less than the demand may result in the loss of clientele.

Dairy farmers or producers shall tend to supply more milk during the flush season when they have a higher marketable surplus but tend to cut down during the lean season when they may get higher prices from other clients.

Hence it is important to enter into an agreement with the farmers about the maximum quantity during the flush season as well as the minimum during lean seasons.

Thus procuring the optimum quantity is a sensitive balance that needs to be maintained for sustained success.

Source of Milk

The right source of collecting is from homegrown farmers, which we have discussed earlier. Due to a lack of experience, information and connections, at times, many mini dairies source the milk from middlemen or semi-organised farmers and may end up with not-so-good quality milk or be forced to pay higher prices.

As discussed earlier, the right source shall vary from place to place and on the conditions prevailing in the area. A righteous decision shall depend upon all the factors like what quality, what price, and what kind of agreement producers are willing to enter into for long-term supply.

For a mini dairy, it is important to have a multitude of sources and not depend on a single source.

Pricing of Milk

There are different systems of pricing milk -the most traditional being quantity-based or litres of milk irrespective of Fat & SNF contents, adulteration with water etc.,. The milk is sold by vendors (Doodhiyas) doing home delivery or by the traditional local dairies.

However, this kind of pricing is detrimental to the dairies processing milk and selling packaged milk.

They have to choose among the various other methods prevalent in the industry, for example, On kgs fat or Kgs SNF or Kgs total solids or dual axis pricing policy considering both Fat & SNF contents to differentiate between Cow and Buffalo Milk.

It may be required to fix a minimum & maximum Fat & SNF levels, and beyond those levels, milk may be rejected or accepted with a penalty, a bonus may be given for A grade quality (based on MBR time), etc.

Understanding how to fix the prices and how to calculate the penalty or the bonus is essential for the success of a dairy entrepreneur. This would be different as per geographical areas.

To summarise, we can say that the collection of substandard or poor quality milk, more than the requirements or less than the market needs, at un-economical prices and from unreliable vendors, will be detrimental to the health of the mini dairy.

Now let me share with you some pro tips on how to build a sound procurement system:

- Build your own network for milk collection, enter into long-term agreements with the milk producers & farmers, assure them of timely payment and bonuses for quality/while penalising them for any deterioration in quality, and above all, establish trust and goodwill with them. The success of the mini dairies depends not only on your processing (we shall learn in the next chapter) but also on your vendors. **As it is said, you can only control the quality and not build it.** If your raw milk is not good, whatever processing one may do, it cannot be improved.

- Hence you also need to educate your producers about the benefits of producing good-quality milk.

- While providing them education & inputs for healthy milk production, you also need to have a system to monitor the quality of milk and ensure that they supply you with the required quantity, quality and at the justified price.

- One also needs to make a decision about cooling the milk at the source (setting up a Bulk Milk Cooler) or collecting raw unchilled milk and transporting it to the milk processing unit. This decision will depend upon the distance and time gap between milk production and processing.

- The cost of collection and transportation to the processing unit is also a factor. Since the milking is done twice a day, traditionally, milk is collected and transported to the processing unit twice a day. This may be advisable if the distance between the two is not much, and it ensures the quality of milk is not being compromised during transportation. The new trend is to install **Bulk Milk Cooling Tanks** at the village level and collect the raw chilled milk once a day by a road milk tanker. A dairy entrepreneur should assess which method of collection would be best suited to their circumstances. To procure raw unchilled or raw chilled milk is a factor determined by the business strategy adopted. There are clients who will pay a premium price only if they are assured that they are getting fresh milk directly from the farm, without any processing, not even cooling. This is more in demand because even pasteurised milk is not used directly by most Indian households, and it is boiled by default. However, maintaining a cold chain would ensure the quality of milk.

- Surveying the villages to collect milk from homegrown farmers and creating a route map of the area is also an important factor so that milk from different locations reaches the processing unit in the shortest time lapse and with the lowest cost per litre of milk.

- It is important for the new entrepreneur to survey the rural area beforehand and find out about the system & pricing of milk prevalent during the year. Else they may be taken for a ride and may end up procuring substandard milk at higher prices which is a readymade recipe for disaster.

- Arriving at the pricing and creating a rate chart, incorporating bonuses & penalties is a valuable tool in the hands of entrepreneurs, and they need to learn it beforehand.

- Lastly, understanding the operations of the milk collection centre so that no one can cheat them on milk collection is also important. How the milk from different farmers is to be accounted for, how it is analysed and how the total amount payable for the milk quantity & quality received is arrived at.

Successful & profitable dairy enterprises are those that have a strong and organised milk procurement system in place. Building a network gives them the power to dominate, be a leader and fix the milk procurement prices, and all else follows.

There is still more to learn, so we need to go more in-depth before you are ready to put all your investment into your dairy enterprise.

Pillar No.3: Milk Processing

Milk processing is primarily a treatment - which could be chemical or mechanical - like adding some additives to the milk or thermal treatment to make the milk safe for consumption and extend its shelf life.

As we are aware, milk is a highly perishable commodity, and if not taken care of, it tends to get sour and curdle on heating.

Two main purposes of milk processing are:

- To increase the keeping quality of milk

- To make it safe for human consumption or conversion into other products.

Before we learn about the processing, we need to know why the milk spoils quickly and what are the Constituents of milk. If we talk of cow milk, it is 87-88% water, and the remaining 12 - 13% are milk solids which consist of Fat, Lactose (Milk sugar or carbohydrate), Milk Protein and minerals & Vitamins.

Being of high nutritive value, it is prone to bacterial spoilage. Immediately after milking as the milk is at body temperature, at 35 deg C. This temperature is optimum for the growth of microorganisms, leading to an increase in acidity, resulting in the souring and curdling of milk.

Hence it implies that any method of processing should be that which shall retard the growth of microorganisms or destroy them. Based on this knowledge, we can now say that various methods of processing which shall preserve the natural quality of milk, enhance its shelf life and used to convert it to products are:

- Cooling of raw milk to a temperature not favourable to the growth of microorganisms, that is, cooling the milk to 4 deg C or lower.

- Pasteurisation of milk - a combination of time & temperature which destroys the pathogenic bacteria completely (safety) and non-pathogens up to 90% (preservation)

- Sterilisation of milk completely destroys all the microorganisms, including spore formers.

- Homogenization of milk,

- Separation of fat to make fat-rich products,

- Fermentation under controlled conditions (Dahi, yoghourt, cheese, etc.) is the other processing technique.

Each process is different and needs different kinds of equipment. It is important to select the right process and the right kind of equipment.

Any processing is a step of operations with certain parameters to accomplish those operations be it cooling or heating or concentration or drying or evaporation, or filtration. We discuss hereunder important processing parameters in relation to the milk and the kind of techniques available that helps in the proper selection of equipment.

Cooling of Milk

As mentioned earlier, cooling of milk is done to control bacterial growth. Microorganisms (bacteria) present in milk have optimum growth at warm temperatures between 35 to 37 deg C. Lower the temperature, the less the bacterial activity. Hence, it takes time for bacteria to spoil the milk. Hence cooling milk helps to control bacterial growth and extend the shelf life of milk. Cooling to 4 deg C is recommended as the bacterial growth is minimised and keeps the milk safe & fresh.

Cooling can be done either by transferring the raw unchilled milk to a cooling tank (called a Bulk Milk Cooler or BMC), wherein it is cooled to 4 deg C. The BMC acts as a storage vessel also. The other way is to rapidly cool the milk by passing it through a heat exchanger and using an external source of a cooling agent, which could be iced water or iced brine or iced glycol is used.

Pasteurization

A time & temperature combination is selected for the process depending upon if it is a batch or continuous, called as Low-Temperature Long Time (LTLT) or High-Temperature Short Time (HTST), respectively. Pasteurisation is not about heating only but also cooling it back to a low temperature so that milk can be handled, packed and checked for the growth of any residual bacteria.

The process selection depends on the milk quantity that is to be pasteurised per day. The selection of equipment should take into consideration the cost of processing per litre of milk as well as the economic efficiency of the process selected. Manually operated or automated machinery choices, monitoring processes and controls are other aspects that must be considered as well.

Standardization of Milk

Standardisation of milk with respect to its Fat & SNF could turn out to be tricky as well as a big drain on the margins if there is no right policy to source the raw milk and it is not compatible with the end products required, For example, if the milk fat is on the lower side, how does one meet the FSSAI requirement? Say the fat is 4.0%, and one wants to sell full cream milk, which will be at least 6.0% fat. This can be done only if two different standard milk is processed - one with low fat, say toned or double toned, that is less than the fat in raw milk and the other with high fat.

Standardising SNF is more tricky as it normally involves increasing the SNF, which can be done by adding the SNF from other ingredients, say SMP (Skimmed Milk Powder). This will add to the cost as prices of SMP keep fluctuating throughout the year. Also, one needs to learn how much SMP is to be added, how to add or avoid it and go for some other method like milk concentration. Every operation adds to the cost.

Hence the importance of standardisation for the right kind of milk or milk products being processed by the dairy is vital. One should fix upper and lower limits on the Fat & SNF levels while formulating the milk procurement policy.

Homogenization of Milk

Many entrepreneurs are unable to decide if they should go for homogenisation or not. It depends upon the marketing strategy and the preference of one's clients. If your clientele mainly consists of housewives looking for thick Malai, go for full cream milk and no homogenization. But if the purpose is to provide richness and better colour to the milk, homogenization is needed. You will also need to take a call on What capacity homogenizer you need. The equipment requires a lot of power and hence adds to the cost.

Manufacturing Products

Each product requires different kinds of processing steps. As mentioned above, the products can be categorised as per the recipe or process.

Entrepreneurs must understand the SOP for manufacturing each product, process parameters and how to monitor them. **Importantly the quality of milk required for each product needs to be understood for sourcing the right kind of milk.**

One must understand that there is no single equipment to manufacture any product but a number of steps to manufacture, and each step has to be religiously followed to manufacture quality products.

We can state that cooling, standardisation and packing the milk in bottles or sachets or any container is also termed processing. This kind of milk is known as **Packed & Chilled Raw Milk.**

Raw milk may be pasteurised, standardised, homogenised or sterilised with or without the addition of sugar, flavours and other permitted ingredients to make milk beverages, or it may be converted to any kind of milk product based on different processing parameters.

The products can probably be classified as Fat based (butter/ghee) or SNF-based (SMP), desiccated (Khoa/rubbery), coagulated (paneer/Chhena/Cheese) or fermented (dahi/lassi/chhaach) or frozen (ice-cream).

Each product requires different kinds of processing lines and equipment. And this determines the success or failure of the dairy enterprise. Selecting the wrong product or inefficient processing line, or choosing the wrong kind of equipment is a sure-shot recipe for disaster.

In a nutshell, a dairy entrepreneur should have in-depth knowledge of milk and milk product processing. Successful and profitable dairy entrepreneurs understand the technologies, processes, best practices, protocols and parameters involved in creating and implementing quality monitoring systems with stringent and consistent controls to enhance the quality of their products while keeping them cost-effective.

They should be well informed of the different operations involved in milk processing. A lot of small dairy entrepreneurs who are in this field many a time do not understand the importance of the standardization process. Hence they incur low profits and have bleak chances of growth. The biggest tool for ensuring quality milk and milk products is the Standardisation of the milk on the basis of Fat and SNF, which ensures uniform quality and also helps in the determination of costing, and hence helps in deciding pricing and profitability of the unit and which-in return gives a consistent quality of output and increased profitability.

Another area that new dairy processing entrepreneurs sometimes tend to undermine is the importance of hygiene in processes. Hygiene is essential to maintaining good quality. You might have come across dairies that have a foul smell. Such dairies continuously struggle to grow. Whereas successful and profitable dairy enterprise owners control and follow stringent hygiene standards in the production processes in a step-by-step manner.

The most important key skill of successful and profitable dairy enterprises is their ability to diagnose the milk quality in every step of production. Hence, one can take all precautionary measures before the merchandise hits the market. Overall the aim is to be in a position to control the supply chain with **Zero Complaints** all across the year.

Pillar No.4: Marketing

The fourth pillar is milk marketing which is the most important and critical in creating successful and profitable dairy enterprises. Many dairy entrepreneurs get trained and do good in quality control, milk procurement and milk processing but fail in milk marketing.

I would say 80% of dairy enterprises struggle mainly because of the absence of assessment and a clear understanding of milk marketing.

Assumptions in Milk Marketing

It is important to have a reality check of the marketing strategy made specifically with respect to your potential clients and market.

The first point of clarity should be whether this has been formulated as per the facts of the market or it is based on assumptions.

Most dairies fail because of poor marketing strategies or no marketing strategy at all or because their marketing strategy is based upon assumptions instead of real data.

New entrepreneurs use their own past experience of their previous industry/sector and make assumptions based on the information available to them or on the basis of their personal consumer needs for milk to build their new dairy enterprise.

To understand and develop a good marketing strategy, you need to dive deep into your designated marketplace to understand its dynamics thoroughly.

- What are the consumers really looking for?
- One must understand whether the product mix you wish to enter the marketplace with, has a demand or if there already exists an inherent choice/demand in your market.
- You need to clearly identify and understand the demand of consumers in your marketplace.
- Is there any gap in demand or supply?

- Are there any taste preferences or new product formulations required?

Deep Dive Analysis of Targeted Consumers:

We need to have a deep dive into the targeted market, which can be done by an individual or a team to understand that whatever marketing strategy or even business plan we are formulating is validated in reality by the market demands and expectations.

By doing this deep dive analysis, we would be able to brainstorm to validate our marketing strategy or see if our product strategy solves the consumer problem or provides us with an idea which could be used in our marketing creations. All this can be achieved by investing in a consumer survey.

Consumer surveys help us understand the present position of our targeted audience or to understand the gaps between what you would like to market and what is in demand. Is there a niche demand that a new dairy enterprise can fulfil? Many new entrants do not spend their time and money investigating their markets; hence they take important decisions based on assumptions, and they fall apart.

Creating Trust

Milk is an everyday commodity used at home daily, and a buyer's decision solely tends towards the trust of the brand and pricing of the product best suited to the buyer's pocket. **India is self-sufficient regarding the availability of milk in most places, so every one has been sourcing from their preferred source of milk. Now, what is it that a new dairy** entrepreneur can do to enhance and speed up the acceptability of their product?

Think of your brand of milk and that of another of your competitors. Both kinds of milk are white, and both kinds of milk are of the same Fat/SNF & same quality. How would you convince the consumer that they should choose your brand?

The most important thing is to understand how you will distinguish your milk from the other brands offered in the market.

For example, there is an existing brand, 'A', which is selling in your market, and you come up with your own brand 'B'. Now my question is, why would a consumer pick your brand 'B'? Unless and until you are not aware and clear about how to distinguish your offerings in the market, you will not even be able to start your marketing in the right direction. A new entrepreneur, especially micro and small and medium dairy entrepreneurs, are not able to distinguish their offering to consumers, or if they do, then they are generally weak and unable to excite consumers to choose their brand. Hence they face tough competition and slow or declining sales unless and until there is no competition at your place of work.

So we need to create our own unique selling proposition in this crowded market.

Remember, if you can create an urge within your customer to pick your brand with your marketing campaigns, then only you will prosper and have chances of growth.

Creating a unique selling proposition would require marketing expertise, which you can do by yourself or by hiring an expert and studying the existing competition and their unique selling propositions prevailing in the market. Also, you must understand what it is that your consumer values in your market and what is your organisational strength. This way, you will be able to create your own USP, and that would add to the foundation of your brand.

When a new entrant comes into a competitive market, the first thing he thinks of is creating an entry with a lower pricing strategy to grab the market share quickly.

This is what most new entrants generally think. But is it correct? Will it help? I would say it would not help, especially for a new entrant, as just competing with bigger players on pricing would not let you sustain for long.

You must remember that the prospective customer may be willing to pay the price for the milk & products based on their perception of the quality and value for money.

The best strategy is to find out what the customer is looking for, position your product accordingly and price it at an optimum value.

Good marketing is the key to creating demand for your product. However, Milk marketing has a totally different perspective than the marketing of other commodities, with the clear distinction that milk is the only product which is purchased by consumers every day and mostly from similar brands and similar variants. There is no other product that has a similar emotional value as milk.

- So, how can you create your own strong brand?

- How can you formulate your marketing strategy?

- How can you decide on a good marketing mix for your company?

- What can you say to customers to differentiate your milk from the other milk available in the market?

- What content would you make for your marketing campaign?

- What would you advertise?

- All the above questions need to be answered in order to formulate a winning marketing strategy for your dairy enterprise.

Digital Marketing

New entrants usually do not have a big advertising budget and don't opt for commercial TV advertising, billboards, newspaper ads, or radio ads because of budgetary constraints. Hence, the only way for a new dairy entrepreneur to reach its target audience, i.e. consumers, is by using digital communication and marketing means.

In today's world, digital marketing is the key to publicising and establishing a brand name.

Marketing through Social media has revolutionised the dynamics of advertising. It has helped to reach target audiences directly and resulted in an increased level of accuracy using special demographics and deploying specific algorithms, all designed to curate a solution and product for the end consumer.

Especially if one is using various E-Commerce channels for a designated geographical area, then using a social media platform would prove to be effective and also help to convert prospective clients and audiences into consumers in all actuality.

Although social media as a communication platform is free, growing and developing your target audience is an expensive affair, even though one might choose organic marketing methodologies.

Paid social media or advertising campaigns, on the other hand, are the aptest ways to convey messages to your target audience as these are customisable and hence create value for money paid in advertising. There are several platforms, such as Facebook, Instagram, Youtube, Twitter, Pinterest, and Google Apps, which have different types of viewers and users.

They would each have their own expense and a completely different strategy which they may prefer to use to create their own digital campaign. One might want to consider different digital marketing agencies and work with them. This would require dispensing a monthly professional fee along with daily expenses or expenditure encouragement and expenditure along with additional daily spending on the campaign, which is usually chargeable by social media platforms.

The biggest trap is that you can easily end up burning your money with no surety of getting the desired results. Getting the desired results from any digital marketing agency requires you to create a good and efficient communication and reporting system to ensure control, evaluation and overall diligence.

This is also necessary to evaluate the performance of the digital marketing agency and the advertising campaign such that it generates the desired results. Otherwise, it does not matter how much you spend on digital campaigns. If you don't have a clear marketing strategy or the right resources to execute the same, or you are not experimenting enough, you will not get the desired results.

The campaigns should be designed such that all the information presented is inspiring and ultimately must lead to a call to action wherein an urge to buy the product is created or engendered. This requires creativity and an "out of the box" thinking paradigm.

Although, some new enterprises have expectations which can be unrealistic and impractical. This usually occurs when the research done is inadequate, and overall there is a lack of understanding of the targeted audience, thus leading to the failure of marketing campaigns.

Now that you have a clear understanding of the challenges as well as the knowledge to firmly erect the 4 pillars that are the foundation of a successful and profitable dairy business, it's time for you to put your learning into practice and start building or expanding your dairy business on to the path of sure-fire success.

Thank you for reading this book. It proves that you are serious about running a successful and profitable dairy. So go ahead, and apply your learnings to establish yourself as a trailblazer in your industry, enjoying the fruits of your labour as profits while contributing to a healthy society.

For those of you who truly wish to be the trailblazers in this sector or those who want to scale up your dairy business to the next level in minimum time, I invite you to be a part of the Dairy Explorer Program, where I will personally handhold you and mentor you onto the path of amazing success and profitability in minimum time with minimum challenges.

To enroll on the Dairy Explorer Program, go here

www.chadha.vip/dxp

To Speak to the Program Manager, you can call

+91-8588844771

Email us: info@chadhasales.com

For more updates and success tips, stay connected with us at

www.facebook.com/chadhasales

www.instagram.com/chadhasales

twitter.com/Chadha_Amardeep

www.youtube.com/user/chadhasales1/videos

www.linkedin.com/in/amardeep-chadha

The Gift

Making the right decisions may be easy for some and may not be so easy for others. So, if you feel you need further support and hand-holding or have questions unanswered, feel free to avail the Free Gift below: facilities that help in providing our customers with consistent quality at all times. The company's R&D Department anticipates future needs and works upon them, which keeps the company miles ahead of others.

Apart from being a front-runner in the domestic market, the company caters to the vast need of the quality-conscious market of the world. The company's Indian clientele includes the National Dairy Development Board, Govt. & Private Milk Co-operatives, Dairy Federations, Dairy Farms, Public Sector Undertakings, Multinational Companies etc.

Our Factories are located at Distt Sonepat, (Haryana), and our Corporate office is centrally located in the Capital of India. Delhi.

The torch has been kept alive and burning by Amardeep Singh Chadha, fuelled by his passion for helping dairy enterprises. This has made him India's #1 Mentor for starting a Dairy Enterprise.

Amardeep Singh Chadha is a proven name in the DAIRY INDUSTRY with 23 years of extensive experience. He coaches budding entrepreneurs and dairy owners to obtain absolute clarity on setting up a new dairy enterprise or managing existing dairy units.

Having invested so many years in the Industry, Mr. Chadha has in-depth practical knowledge in the area of Milk Quality, Milk Collection, Milk Processing, and Milk Marketing and has first-hand experience with the issues faced in the dairy industry. His Strategic interventions help his mentees attain confidence and create a practical path for their dairy business.

Today we proudly declare that we are in the business of improving the quality and profitability of the dairy business, and we are committed to continuing to do so for eternity in new and innovative ways.

Our Story

Like every successful story, ours is built on the twin pillars of utmost passion and strong determination.

Sardar Makhan Singh Chadha ran a small-scale dairy in pre-partition Punjab. When the tribulations of partition hit India, he moved to Delhi from Pakistan.

Then began a journey of starting everything from nothing. With his grit & determination, coupled with his charm and positive attitude, he started delivering milk on a rented bicycle.

Soon he progressed to a small dairy at the Tis Hazari Refugee Camp.

Things took a turn for the business when this ingenious entrepreneur single-handedly imported the Gerber Centrifuge, a milk-testing instrument from Switzerland with little technical training and capital.

The Gerber centrifuge proto-type at that time caught the attention of many other dairy owners. And the visionary became a manufacturer of dairy machinery from a mere supplier of dairy products.

Along with his two sons - Mohinder Paul Singh Chadha and Baldev Singh Chadha, he expanded the business with the production of various machinery and equipment like Cream Separators, Milk Testing Appliances, Lockstoppers, Butyrometers, Aluminium Alloy Milk Cans, and Milk Cooling Tanks.

The legacy has been taken forward by three brothers, Manjeet, Amardeep and Jagdeep. Today, as the pioneers of dairy machinery and equipment, Chadha Sales Pvt. Ltd. is one of the most trusted names in the industry. And together with the new generation, we strive to keep innovating to give our customers the best service possible.

Chadha Sales Private Ltd is a pioneer company in the field of Dairy Equipment and Plants. The Company has grown from a micro-enterprise to a large company with customers all across the globe.

Chadha Sales Pvt. Ltd is backed by a professional team of skilled and experienced engineers. The company has a well-equipped in-house production unit with state-of-the-art machines.

There are a number of inspection instruments and testing facilities that help in providing our customers with consistent quality at all times. The company's R&D Department anticipates future needs and works upon them, which keeps the company miles ahead of others.

Apart from being a front-runner in the domestic market, the company caters to the vast need of the quality-conscious market of the world. The company's Indian clientele includes the National Dairy Development Board, Govt. & Private Milk Co-operatives, Dairy Federations, Dairy Farms, Public Sector Undertakings, Multinational Companies etc.

Our Factories are located at Distt Sonepat, (Haryana), and our Corporate office is centrally located in the Capital of India. Delhi.

The torch has been kept alive and burning by Amardeep Singh Chadha, fuelled by his passion for helping dairy enterprises. This has made him India's #1 Mentor for starting a Dairy Enterprise.

Amardeep Singh Chadha is a proven name in the DAIRY INDUSTRY with 23 years of extensive experience. He coaches budding entrepreneurs and dairy owners to obtain absolute clarity on setting up a new dairy enterprise or managing existing dairy units.

Having invested so many years in the Industry, Mr. Chadha has in-depth practical knowledge in the area of Milk Quality, Milk Collection, Milk Processing, and Milk Marketing and has first-hand experience with the issues faced in the dairy industry. His Strategic interventions help his mentees attain confidence and create a practical path for their dairy business.

Today we proudly declare that we are in the business of improving the quality and profitability of the dairy business, and we are committed to continuing to do so for eternity in new and innovative ways.